HOLIDAY SIDE HUSTLE

The Q4 Sales Success Manual for Small Business Owners

BY

KARI R. TAYLOR

Table of Contents

Introduction

Managing the fourth quarter sales season

Chapter 1

Establishing the Scene - Getting Ready for the Holiday Rush

Chapter 2

Creating a Winning Marketing Plan

Chapter 3

Choosing the Right Products

Chapter 4

Optimizing Personnel and Training for Performance

Chapter 5

Inventory and fulfillment management

Chapter 6

Increasing Customer Satisfaction

Chapter 7

Post-Holiday Assessment and Future Planning

Chapter 8

20 Lucrative Business Start-Up Choices

Conclusion

Making a Plan for Eternal Success

Introduction:

Managing the fourth quarter sales season

In the world of business, the fourth quarter of the year serves as the battlefield when businesses slug it out for customers' attention as well as money. Seasonally, there are many opportunities, but there are also many difficulties. Nevertheless, I am here in front of you as proof that it is feasible for businesses to not only navigate but also grow at this crucial time of the year, despite all the challenges and fierce competition.

My experience as a small business owner has been characterized by both highs and lows related to success and hardship. I had to contend with tenacious rivals, shifting market dynamics, and the arduous task of satisfying growing client demands throughout the holiday season. I've gained insightful knowledge from it all, which has helped me not only survive the storms but also come out on top.

The knowledge and understanding I'll impart in this book isn't just a record of my own experiences; it's also an outline of steps that will enable you to successfully navigate and complete your own Q4 sales season. You will learn that, like me, you can produce great outcomes, even in the face of fierce competition, provided you adhere to the tactics and ideas described in these pages.

The corporate environment may be brutally competitive, especially during the holidays. Standing apart is essential because so many businesses are competing for the same group of customers. We will go deeply into the art of difference in the chapters that follow, highlighting the significance of a differentiating feature that makes your company stand out from the competition. You will discover how to create a successful marketing plan, maximize your product choices, and provide a remarkable customer experience that leaves a positive impression.

This book is intended to be your go-to resource for useful guidance, insightful suggestions, and a wealth of time-tested strategies. I sincerely believe that you, as the owners of small businesses and as thriving entrepreneur, have the ability to not only survive but also prosper during the Q4 sales season. I'm excited to share my skills and experiences with you because I believe that your businesses will gain a great deal from the lessons I've learned.

Therefore let's set out on this trip collectively, armed with the techniques and tactics required to make this Q4 your best one yet. The road may be difficult, but with tenacity, creativity, and the advice in this book, you can succeed in sales that will have a long-lasting impact on your company and your potential business ventures.

8

Chapter 1

Establishing the Scene - Getting Ready for the Holiday Rush

In 2016, as the peak of the holiday season drew near, I discovered myself in a precarious position. Even though my tiny firm has experienced its share of ups and downs, the holiday rush posed a special difficulty. It was a decisive moment that would either take my company to new heights or cause it to struggle to stay competitive. That crucial year's events would influence how I would approach the holiday shopping seasons for years to come.

It's crucial to stand back and think deeply before getting down to the nitty-gritty of holiday preparations. I started out by reviewing the triumphs and flops of recent holiday seasons. What has been successful? What didn't live up to requirements? I was able to find trends and cycles that will guide my future strategy thanks to this retrospective exercise.

The necessity of having a clearly defined comprehensive plan in place was one of the most important lessons learned from that tragic year. I came to understand that tackling the holiday rush carelessly would be disastrous. I therefore set out to develop a thorough plan that covered every facet of my business. I had to make sure I had adequate product to satisfy the increased demand, which prompted thorough **evaluation of my inventory**. I discovered the hard way that selling out of in-demand things around the holidays might be really expensive.

Another important factor that I considered was in the area of **staffing**. I made an effort to ensure that they were capable of handling the increase of customers and uphold the kind of service my business was known for, I hired seasonal labor in advance and gave them training.

Drafting out a **marketing plan** was another criteria I considered if I must standing out. I significantly overhauled my marketing approach. I created a marketing campaign for the holidays that not only emphasized my products but also played on the sentimental part of the occasion. Customers responded favorably to this strategy, which helped me stand out from the competitors.

In 2016, I understood that if I must survive, I must flow with the recent tide of the era. I understood how digital the world has turned out to be. I had to do something different, and I called it my **step up plan**. I became aware of how **technology** may speed up holiday preparations. Technology gave me tools to work more efficiently rather than more laboriously, from inventory tracking software to online advertising platforms. I was able to devote more time and resources to important tasks, including choosing products and engaging customers, after I adopted automation. This prompted me to register for A Customer Relationship Management and an online Digital Marketing Training Course. I may have suffered delay in growth in times past, but I made up my mind to do everything possible to equip myself intellectually, to be able to withstand the competitive space and increase sales.

"Understand the difference between working smart and working hard. The results depict the difference. Working hard does not guarantee more results".

Beyond the practical parts of planning, I realized how crucial it was to make my actual store seem celebratory. I enhanced the shopping experience by furnishing the area, playing holiday music, and providing seasonal goodies. These thoughtful details made clients feel at home and enticed them to stay and explore.

IT IS TIME TO TAKE THE STEP TO RETAIN YOUR AUDIENCE!

ACQUIRE THE SKILL AND IMPLEMENT IT.

A Comprehensive Guide to Preparing Your Small Business for a Prosperous Festive Season.

Step 1: Start by thinking back on previous holiday seasons. Determine what went right and wrong. Analyze your difficulties, customer comments, and sales statistics. Your future decisions will be influenced by your understanding of your past.

Step 2: State your goals for the Christmas season. Think about the goals you have for brand awareness, customer happiness, and sales targets. Setting clear objectives will enable you to stay motivated and assess your progress.

Step 3: Thoroughly evaluate your inventory. Make a list of your best-selling items and look for any supply gaps. To guarantee you have enough supplies to fulfill the growing demand over the holidays, place your order early.

Step 4: Plan well in advance for your personnel needs if you need to, hire seasonal workers and make sure they have the proper training so they can help clients. Consider providing your current personnel with cross-training so they can handle several roles amid the busy period.

Step 5: Create a marketing strategy that is specific to the holiday in step five. Both offline and online strategies should be covered in this. To engage your audience, take into account conducting special promotions, producing holiday-themed content, and using social media.

Step 6: Optimize your website for Christmas sales. Make sure it's responsive to mobile devices, loads quickly, and has the most recent product listings. To prevent cart abandonment, implement a simple and user-friendly checkout procedure.

Step 7: Invest in technologies that can help you organize your business. Utilize email marketing systems to automate communication, software for inventory oversight to track stock levels, and analytics tools to real-time monitor performance.

Step 8: Create a cheerful mood in your actual store, if you have one. Create a festive atmosphere, play holiday music, and serve seasonal foods. Encourage customers to visit by involving them in special in-store activities or incentives.

Step 9: Communicate with your customers frequently and early. Send them mailings with a seasonal theme, provide sneak peeks of your Christmas merchandise, and make tailored recommendations based on their past purchases.

Step 10: Be ready for unforeseen difficulties. Create a backup plan in case of problems like staffing shortages or supply chain disruptions. Being adaptable to shifting conditions requires flexibility.

Step 11: Keep track of your advancement all during the Christmas season. Track sales, internet traffic, and consumer behavior with analytics. You should be prepared to make changes immediately if anything isn't working.

Step 12: After the holiday season is over, evaluate your performance in detail. Evaluate your outcomes to your original objectives. What was successful, and what may be improved for the next year? Modify your approach for the coming year using these findings and you will be well on your way to laying the groundwork for a good holiday season if you stick to these guidelines. Always be prepared and flexible if you want to succeed at this challenging time of year.

Chapter 2

Creating a Winning Marketing Plan

Success over the Christmas season and beyond, developing a successful marketing strategy is unquestionably essential. Let me share with you the lessons I've learnt from past errors and the reasons why a well-thought-out marketing strategy is a must in the cutthroat business environment of today. I committed the serious sin of failing to have a thorough holiday marketing plan in the early years of my company. I believed that the season's inherent demand would be sufficient to increase my sales to unpForrecedented heights. I was completely in error. This is a path that I do not wish you to journey through, as it leads to futility and eventually, a dead-end.

I lost out on several opportunities to interact with potential consumers because I lacked a defined plan. My sales fell as a result of my brand getting lost in the wave of Christmas advertising. I observed as other businesses that had well worked out their marketing strategies reaped the benefits while my own struggled.

It is pertinent for you to Understanding the Vital Importance of a Marketing Strategy. Strategy is a technique. It helps you distinct your brand from the others and also helps to map out a unique style and scope for your business. What is your route? What is your style? What is your system? How well have you positioned your business in other to be noticed by prospective customers? What special touch does your business have? How is your brand and packaging like? What problem are you solving? What is the solution you intend to adopt? What style can you adopt that can help retain your customers?

To answer this questions, you must first put yourself in the position of your customers. Define the problem and think like them. So, take your time to ruminate over those questions. Do not be in a hurry to proffer answers.

My early failures taught me an important lesson that in today's business environment, having a solid marketing strategy is not an option, but rather a requirement. This is why:

1. During the Holiday season, the market is oversaturated with goods and services. And you can only stand out from the competition by using a strong marketing plan. It enables you to explain your distinct value proposition to prospective clients, giving them a justification for selecting your brand over rivals. Adopt a solid **DIFFERENTIATION** plan.

2. Strategy helps you Recognize your **Target audience**. A well-thought-out approach can help you identify and connect with your target audience more successfully. You can concentrate your efforts and resources on people who are most likely to become devoted consumers rather than casting a wide net, which will cause a distraction for you.

3. Strategy stirs up your **Consistency level**. It gives your marketing initiatives a road map. By making sure that your branding, messaging, and promotions are consistent across all media, you can give customers a seamless and memorable experience.

4. You can more easily adjust to shifting market conditions and customer trends if you have a strategy in place. You'll have the freedom to change your strategy as necessary to remain current and competitive. You adapt

to any changing condition and still come out strong.

5. By developing a plan, you may deploy your resources effectively. By determining the most cost-effective marketing channels and strategies, you can make sure that every dollar invested yields the highest possible return on investment.

6. Clear goals and key performance indicators are part of a strategic strategy. This implies that you may evaluate the effectiveness of your campaigns, determine what is effective, and make decisions based on data to enhance your outcomes.

Designing a Winning Marketing Plan

Start a successful holiday marketing campaign by doing the following:

1. Decide what you want to accomplish during the holidays, such as boosting sales, raising brand awareness, or increasing consumer interaction. Draft out specific goals to be your road map.

2. Know your target market inside and out. What are their inclinations, problems, and purchasing patterns over the holidays?

3. Determine which marketing channels connect with your audience the most. Social networking, email marketing, content marketing, and paid advertising are a few examples.

4. Create captivating holiday-themed material that relates to the needs and emotions of your

audience. Ensure that it is consistent with the messaging and values of your brand.

5. To save time and guarantee consistency, plan your marketing calendar and automate repetitive processes.

6. Keep a close eye on your campaigns and be prepared to make changes in response to real-time data. It's possible that what works in week one won't in week four.

You may avoid the traps I ran into in my early career and set up your company for success in the cutthroat world of Christmas sales by devoting time and effort to creating a strong marketing strategy. Keep in mind that the appropriate strategy not only increases revenue but also fosters strong client relationships that will help your business long after the holiday season has passed.

HOLIDAY HUSTLE

26

YOUR REALISTIC TO-DO LIST

Earlier than the holiday season

> ➢ Establish Specific, Measurable Goals - Establish clear objectives for the holiday season, such as a 20% increase in sales or a 15% increase in email subscribers.

> ➢ Carry out market research to learn about the tastes, actions, and purchasing patterns of your target market.

> ➢ Select the best marketing channels for your target market (such as paid advertising, email marketing, social media, and content marketing).

Prior to the holiday season, by many months

> ➤ 4. Make a content calendar that specifies the kind of content you'll publish in the weeks leading up to and during the holidays.

> ➤ 5. Distribute your marketing money among various platforms and initiatives while keeping in mind your objectives and anticipated return on investment.

Two to three months prior to the holiday season

> ➤ Produce Holiday-related material that is in line with the messaging of your business and appeals to your audience. This could involve email campaigns, blog postings, or social media updates.

➢ Install applications that can help you automate your marketing initiatives, such as scheduling social media postings and email campaigns.

Just One Month before the Holiday's

➢ Create visually appealing visuals and creative elements for your marketing initiatives, such as graphics, photos, and videos.

➢ To make your email marketing efforts more individualized, all you need to do is to segment your email list based on client preferences, past purchases, or other pertinent variables.

A few weeks before the holidays

➢ Start implementing your holiday marketing campaigns using the channels you've selected, such as unique promotions, prizes, or competitions.

➢ Use analytics tools to regularly assess how well your marketing strategies are performing. Determine what is effective working and what needs to be changed, so as to guarantee progress.

Over the course of the holiday season

➢ Use social media to interact with your audience and swiftly respond to customer inquiries. Establish connections and trust.

➢ Constantly improve your marketing initiatives using data that is current. As necessary, modify your budget allocation and plan.

After the holiday season

➢ Carefully assess how well your holiday marketing campaign performed. Match results to your original objectives.

➢ List the successes and failures of the Christmas season. Improve your approach for the upcoming year using these ideas.

➢ Start making plans for the upcoming holiday season, taking into account the lessons you've learned and modifying your plan as necessary. Do not wait until raining season before you start planting your seeds. Now is the time to plan, if you must continue to survive.

You'll be well-equipped to develop and implement a successful marketing strategy for the holiday season and beyond if you stick to this task list. Keep in mind that a well-planned and implemented marketing campaign can significantly impact the growth of your business during this crucial time of the year.

CREATE ONE NOW BEFORE YOU BEGIN THE NEXT CHAPTER

Chapter 3

Choosing the Right Products

In my experience as a small business owner, there was a turning point that I'd want to share with you since it demonstrated the enormous potential of correctly optimized product selection. It took me some time to understand the importance of this idea, but once I did, my company underwent a growth transformation I could not have possibly predicted.

I chose my products in the early years of my company in a fairly arbitrary manner. I would keep a large range of goods in store because I believed that giving customers a lot of options would inevitably result in a diverse clientele. Although this method had certain advantages, it soon became clear that it was not a viable one, particularly during the Christmas season.

My efforts to control inventories and deliver the caliber of customer service I desired left me drowning in a sea of items. Despite the bustle of activity, it was a stressful and intimidating experience, and my sales figures didn't accurately reflect the work I was putting in. There has to be a change.

I had a lightbulb moment during a particularly difficult holiday season. I came to the conclusion that having the most comprehensive product catalog was not necessary for success in retail, especially during moments of high sales. It all came down to having the appropriate products that spoke to my target market. I set out on a quest to improve and streamline my method of choosing products.

You too can learn How to experience the wonder of properly tailored product selection by:

1. Getting to Know Your Audience Well:

Spending time getting to know your target market would do you a great deal of help. Find out what their shopping habits, needs, and preferences are. Discover these, and you can cater your product assortment to their preferences if you are intimately familiar with your clients. Know their taste and they will keep coming for more when you deliver the best.

2. Recognize seasonal trends and top sellers:

- Examine your historical sales data to pinpoint your top-performing goods. During the holiday season, these products should continue to sell strongly. Keep an eye out for seasonal patterns and try to predict what will be in great demand.

3. Curate a Holiday Collection with Specificity.

- Create a targeted assortment of products that are in line with the Christmas season and the preferences of your audience rather than attempting to provide everything under the sun. This not only makes it easier for you to manage your inventory but also makes it simpler for your clients to shop.

4. Quality over Quantity

- Prioritize the quality of your product over the quantity. Offering a variety of high-quality, well picked products can frequently result in more client loyalty and pleasure. The quality of your product says a lot about you to your prospective customers. I understand that the economy might at a point be unfriendly, but you must try to maintain your quality at all cost.

5. Optimize Pricing and Profit Margins

- Carefully choose your product's price to ensure that it is both competitive and has a sound profit margin. Keep an eye on the prices of your rivals, but avoid engaging in price competition as this could hurt your profitability. Do not be greedy.

6. Marketing and Promotion

- Through your marketing initiatives, highlight your carefully picked seasonal assortment. To highlight the value and advantages of your items, create appealing product descriptions and employ eye-catching images.

7. Track and Modify

- Keep an eye on how your chosen products are performing. Consider altering your inventory or marketing tactics if some products are not selling as anticipated.

8. Customer feedback and insights

- Pay attention to customer reviews and comments. Utilize this helpful information to narrow down your product selection and pinpoint potential improvement areas.

My business was completely altered after I realized the power of correctly tailored product selection. It dramatically increased revenue and customer happiness in addition to streamlining operations and inventory management. Keep in mind that having the correct products that appeal to your audience and fulfill their holiday needs is more important than simply having the most products.

HOLIDAY HUSTLE

39

YOUR REALISTIC TO-DO LIST

Before The Holiday Season

> ➢ Conduct rigorous audience research to fully comprehend the tastes, needs, and habits of your target market.

> ➢ Examine past sales figures to determine your top-selling items and any seasonal patterns.

Few Months Before the holiday season

> ➢ Create a well-focused assortment of Christmas products based on your audience research and sales statistics.

➢ Check the products you've chosen to see if they live up to or beyond client expectations in terms of quality.

Marketing and Pricing

➢ Establish prices for your holiday products that are both competitive and profitable. Think about elements including price, pricing from competitors, and perceived value.

➢ Develop a marketing strategy that emphasizes your carefully picked seasonal selection. For marketing materials, create eye-catching product descriptions and illustrations.

Over the course of the holiday season

➢ Track the performance of your chosen products on a continuous basis by monitoring sales and customer feedback. Pay a very close attention to your clients comments and reviews. A vital process that must not be ignored.

➢ Adjust as required - Be prepared to modify your product choice in light of sales results and consumer feedback. Restocking high-demand items could be a better option than removing slow-moving items.

You'll be better prepared to choose your products wisely for the Holiday season and increase sales and customer happiness if you adhere to this task list. It's important to keep in mind that having the correct products in stock that suit the tastes of your target market and the holiday spirit is just as important as having a vast inventory.

HOLIDAY HUSTLE

43

Chapter 4

Optimizing Personnel and Training for Performance

Staffing and training for optimal performance is a crucial part of my experience as a small business owner that had a significant impact on the success of my company. In addition to benefiting my firm, investing in my people and giving them the tools they needed to succeed sparked increased performance and passion that spread throughout the entire organization.

I had the key insight early in my entrepreneurial path that my employees weren't just laborers; they were the face of my company. Their contacts with customers, product expertise, and excitement all had a direct impact on how people saw my brand.

I made the decision to drastically alter my strategy for hiring and training new employees. It wasn't just about filling roles; it was also about developing a team that was enthusiastic about our offerings and dedicated to providing first-rate service.

I have met a few business owners who claim it is a waste of time to equip their staffs, as they believe they might decide to resign when they get bigger offers elsewhere. Even though at the initial stage I agreed with him, but the truth is that, when you treat your staffs fairly enough, empower them and regard them, they are likely to give their best to ensuring you get the result of the impact you have invested on them. They are your face, your first brand outside the four walls of your organization. They tell a lot about what your business represent. Build them and watch how it reflects on the growth of your business.

To achieve results in your business setup, you can implement these:

1. Spend time finding the best candidates. Look for people that not only possess the appropriate qualifications but also share your passion for your offerings and your company's goals.

2. Create a thorough training program that gives your personnel in-depth product knowledge and top-notch customer service abilities. Ensure that they are aware of the mission and values of your brand.

3. Give your employees the freedom to own up to their duties. Encourage them to make suggestions for changes and new ideas that could improve the customer experience. Give them room

to express themselves. This will save you the stress of carrying out all the planning responsibilities alone. Never underestimate the idea of any man.

4. Training doesn't end with onboarding. Provide opportunities for ongoing learning to keep your personnel informed about new goods and market developments. To create a versatile team, think about cross-training.

5. Congratulate yourself for a job well done. This can be accomplished through rewards, incentives, or even just verbal praise. A high-performing team is one that is motivated.

6. Foster an atmosphere of free communication. Ask your staff for input on their experiences and

difficulties on a regular basis. Their observations may result in beneficial advancements.

7. As a company owner, your passion and commitment set the tone for your staff. Show your commitment to quality and your love for your products by setting an example for others.

8. Foster a healthy workplace culture where employees feel appreciated and driven. Encourage cooperation, teamwork, and a sense of community.

The Impact of Ripples on Your Business

Investing in peak performance hiring and training makes it evident that your company appreciates excellence. Your staff members feel the same way about this dedication to quality, and they express it in their dealings with clients.

Your employees progress from being just workers to brand ambassadors. They have the expertise and zeal to direct consumers toward the greatest items and deliver first-rate service. This establishes a positive feedback loop where happy clients turn into devoted clients, increasing sales and business development.

In essence, developing your staff is the same as developing your company. They are an essential component of your product line and have a big impact on how customers are treated as a whole. The foundation for peak performance, contagious excitement, and long-term business success is laid when you give them the freedom to work at their highest potential.

HOLIDAY HUSTLE

YOUR REALISTIC TO-DO LIST

Selection and Recruitment

➤ Clearly define the essential qualities and features you are looking for in candidates, putting a focus on a shared love for your goods and brand.

➤ Craft job descriptions that not only describe job duties but also communicate your company's mission and values in order to draw applicants who share your vision.

Complete Guidance

➤ Produce thorough training materials that go over product knowledge, best practices for customer service, and your company's core principles.

➤ Create a structured onboarding procedure to acquaint new hires with the values, guidelines, and expectations of your business.

Responsibility and Independence

➤ Promote a sense of ownership and responsibility among your personnel by encouraging and empowering them to make decisions relevant to their responsibilities.

➤ Establish avenues for workers to submit ideas and improvements. Take action on wise recommendations to increase morale and output.

Continual Improvement

➢ To keep your team up to date, provide continual training and development opportunities, such as workshops, seminars, and online courses.

➢ Put cross-training programs into place to increase employee skill sets and build a flexible team.

Acknowledgement and Compensation

➢ Create recognition programs that recognize and honor exceptional performance, whether by way of bonuses, rewards, or public acclaim.

> Conduct regular performance assessments to offer constructive criticism and establish objectives for improvement.

Employee Evaluation

> Establish an evaluation-friendly workplace where staff members feel free to share their views and experiences.

> Respond to employee review by taking appropriate action to address issues, make required adjustments, and demonstrate that their input is valued.

Set a Good Example

➢ Set a positive example by showcasing your love for your goods and dedication to excellence in your own work.

For Optimal Working Conditions

➢ Create a supportive workplace through team-building exercises, transparent communication, and an appreciation-based culture.

➢ Encourage teamwork and collaboration among your employees. A cohesive team can provide superior results.

Chapter 5

Inventory and fulfillment management

Two essential components of efficient business operations that are occasionally neglected or undervalued are inventory management and fulfillment. It's a common blunder that many business owners fail to handle with the thoroughness it requires. However, adopting proactive and methodical steps in this area can significantly improve your company's productivity, client satisfaction, and bottom line. I've personally experienced the effects of ignoring inventory and fulfillment procedures. Early on in my entrepreneurial career, I too miscalculated the significance of these crucial tasks. As a result, my company faced a variety of difficulties:

Commodities where Overstocked and Understocked. And as a result of poor inventory control, I frequently found myself with a great deal of slow-moving commodities on hand while running out on sought-after goods during periods of high demand. Customers became frustrated and disappointed when things were out of stock, which hurt my brand's reputation and resulted in lost sales chances. This resulted in Financial Stress, as Ineffective inventory control locked up valuable money in surplus stock, impacting cash flow and reducing expansion potential.

Another challenge I had was functional inefficiencies. As there was delay in order shipment caused by inefficient fulfillment procedures. This further damaged consumer confidence and contentment.

The Importance of Inventory and Fulfillment

Effective inventory and fulfillment management is a strategic necessity, not just an issue of operational effectiveness. Here is why it's important:

1. On-time order fulfillment and precise inventory levels support a great customer experience that encourages loyalty and repeat business.

2. Effective inventory management reduces carrying costs, such as capital invested in unsold goods and storage space.

3. You can increase earnings by maximizing sales opportunities and minimizing stock outs and overstock conditions.

4. Administrative Effectiveness: Improving order accuracy, reducing errors, and lowering operational costs are all benefits of streamlining fulfillment procedures.

How to Manage Inventory and Order Fulfillment Effectively in Practice

Take into account the following actionable steps to prevent the risks of ignoring inventory and fulfillment:

1. Make an investment in inventory management software. Use this software to keep track of stock levels, predict demand, and automate reordering procedures.

2. Conduct frequent audits of your inventory to ensure the correctness of your stock records and to quickly spot inconsistencies.

3. To cause restocking orders when inventory reaches a predetermined level, establish reorder points for each product.

4. If it is possible for your company, think about using a JIT (Just in Time) inventory strategy to minimize surplus stock and save carrying costs.

5. Streamline your order fulfillment procedure by automating processes, setting up your warehouse for efficiency, and instructing employees on how to make mistakes as little as possible.

6. To take advantage of their knowledge and infrastructure, think about outsourcing your fulfillment to a 3PL (Third Party Logistics) service provider.

7. Review sales and inventory data frequently to spot patterns, sluggish sellers, and areas for development.

8. To effectively forecast demand, use previous sales data and industry patterns. This can help you make wise inventory decisions.

9. Keep the lines of communication open between your fulfillment and sales teams to make sure they are coordinated and prepared to handle changes in demand.

You can avoid the errors that beset many firms and develop a streamlined, effective, and customer-focused operation by exercising rigorous activities in inventory and fulfillment management. Never undervalue this fundamental component of company success.

YOUR REALISTIC TO-DO LIST

Inventory Control

- ➢ To start, carefully evaluate your present inventory to determine what you have on hand.
- ➢ Do your homework, select the inventory management software option that best meets your company's demands, and put it into practice.
- ➢ Choose reorder points for your goods to prompt restocking orders.
- ➢ Conduct routine inventory audits to check your records' accuracy and physical stock levels.
- ➢ To effectively predict customer demand and help with inventory decisions, use previous sales data and industry trends.

Service Level Optimization

➢ Review your order fulfillment procedures to look for bottlenecks and places that can be improved.

➢ Set up your warehouse for efficiency, making sure that the products are clearly labeled and simple to find.

➢ Educate your personnel on effective order processing, and keep lines of communication open between the fulfillment and sales teams.

➢ If it suits your company's requirements, research outsourcing fulfillment to a third-party logistics (3PL) supplier.

➢ Review sales and inventory data on a regular basis to spot patterns and potential areas for improvement.

➢ To reduce costs associated with carrying, consider using a Just-in-Time (JIT) inventory strategy.

Permanent Management

- For reference and analysis, keep thorough records of inventory levels, orders, and fulfillment procedures.
- Keep your inventory records current to reflect current supply levels.
- Endeavour to be open and honest when informing customers about the availability of products and shipment schedules.
- Regularly evaluate the success of your inventory and fulfillment strategy and make any improvements.
- You may improve inventory management, speed the fulfillment process, and subsequently boost customer happiness and your company's bottom line by adhering to this straightforward must-do list.

HOLIDAY HUSTLE

65

Chapter 6

Increasing Customer Satisfaction

My company strategy has always been centered on maximizing the client experience. It's important to build enduring relationships with customers in addition to simply selling items. In spite of strong competition, I have managed to keep clients by continually focusing on improving their experience. I have also seen them come back again and time again, along with an uninterrupted supply of new ones. Allow me to reveal some of the strategies I used and the important lessons I discovered along this journey.

Putting the consumer at the center of all we do by developing a customer-centric culture was one of the guiding concepts I adopted. Every part of our organization, from developing products to customer assistance, is infused with this attitude. We make an effort to comprehend the wants and needs of our clients, and our actions demonstrate a dedication to fulfilling and surpassing their expectations.

Every client engagement, in our opinion, presents a chance to establish rapport and trust. We want to make every connection feel personal and important, whether it's a warm welcome, tailored product recommendations, or quick answers to questions.

Going the additional mile was a further tactic we employed. Going above and above is frequently the secret to producing unforgettable encounters, according to our research. We continually look for methods to surpass expectations rather than just meeting them. This could entail surprising clients with unanticipated benefits, providing extra help, or making special offers.

Example from My Customers feedback Week

I'd like to present a special instance from our annual Client Evaluation Week to demonstrate the impact of our customer-centric strategy. We collect consumer feedback during this particular week and express our gratitude by giving out free items and discounts. YOU TOO CAN ADOPT IT.

A group of long-term clients who had provided feedback to us the previous year. When asked why customers kept using our goods and services, they cited the following reasons:

1. **Reputability:** Many people expressed a high sense of trust in our brand. They trusted us because we continuously kept our word, and their faith in us grew over time.

2. **Personalized Service**: Several clients praised our capacity to comprehend their

particular requirements and preferences. They valued the individualized product suggestions and the perception that we actually cared about their happiness.

3. **Consistency**: The quality of the products, the level of customer service, and the entire experience all have to be consistent. Their devotion was greatly influenced by the fact that they knew they could count on us.

4. **Community involvement**: People appreciated and recognized the work we did to create a feeling of community around our brand. Customers valued our participation in forums, social media, and gatherings where we helped them connect.

Gaining a Little by Losing a Little

We've frequently been ready to invest more than what might seem immediately advantageous in order to maximize the client experience. However, we are adamant that this commitment to loyalty and trust is a long-term move that pays off. In the near term, it's comparable to "losing a little" in order to "gain abundance" in the shape of long-lasting client connections, personal recommendations, and a solid brand reputation.

Our company has been created on the principle of **Earning Trust**. We've discovered that when consumers believe in a brand, they not only buy more, but also recommend it to others. Additionally, advocates are the real cash in the commercial world. The only way to increase your net worth is through trust, and it only takes a little bit of time to earn it.

We have not only kept customers but also experienced organic growth above and above our projections by continually concentrating on improving the customer experience, building trust, and offering outstanding value. Its evidence of the value of fostering relationships and making client pleasure a priority in your fundamental business strategy.

YOUR REALISTIC TO-DO LIST

Client-Centered Culture

> ➢ Consistently evaluate and comprehend the requirements, preferences, and problems of your customers.
> ➢ Make sure that everyone on your team is committed to the customer-centric strategy across the board.

Individualized Communications

> ➢ Personalize communications with clients by addressing them by name, suggesting products they might like, or sending them a follow-up message.
> ➢ Strive for rapid and useful responses to client enquiries, problems, and concerns.

Going Above and Beyond

➤ Constantly look for methods to provide your consumers with value that goes above and beyond what is anticipated.

➤ To express gratitude and create memorable encounters, think about adding surprise offers, special benefits, or little presents.

Customer Feedback and Participation

➤ To determine client attitude, establish recurring feedback collection tools, such as surveys or feedback forms.

➤ Annual Client Assessment Week - To express thanks and foster participation, plan an annual event that focuses on customer feedback, recognition, and giveaways.

Creating Trust

- ➢ Maintain Consistency in Product and Service Quality - Your products, customer service, and in general customer experience should all be of consistently high quality.
- ➢ Interact with your clients on social media, on forums, or at gatherings that help them feel like they are a part of a community.

Long-Term Goals

- ➢ Investment in Trust - Adopt the perspective that "losing a little" in the near future. Will "gain abundance" in long-term consumer loyalty and brand reputation.
- ➢ Support Building - Recognize that building trust results in consumer advocacy, which over time may be a potent engine for corporate expansion.

HOLIDAY HUSTLE

75

Chapter 7

Post-Holiday Assessment and Future Planning

Please allow me to share a key point in my entrepreneurial path when I realized the significant value of post-holiday introspection and future planning. This approach resulted in a positive and enormous transformation that not only helped my firm advance but also provided me with priceless knowledge about its possibilities for expansion.

In the early stages of my firm, the time following the holidays was frequently accompanied by tiredness and a sense of relief that the busy time had passed. Without really reflecting on what had happened, I was going to require a break, replenishing shelves and taking care of daily tasks. It was only a period of rest and planning for the upcoming year.

To change things up, though, and out of a persistent curiosity, I made the decision to do so one year. I started a thorough post-holiday evaluation. Deep data analysis, customer input, and operational lessons from the most recent holiday season were all parts of the process. This study revealed information that was absolutely nothing short of eye-opening.

Analysis and Insights' Effect

1. I was better able to identify which products had outperformed the competition throughout the holiday season using data analysis. With the use of this knowledge, I was able to choose the right products and manage my inventory for the future year using data.

2. I also combed through customer reviews and feedback, learning important details about their preferences, wants, and trouble issues. This gave me the opportunity to customize my services and raise client satisfaction.

3. The investigation identified several areas that need logistical upgrades, from optimizing fulfillment procedures to improving marketing initiatives.

Making Future Plans

With the information I learned from the post-holiday assessment, I started a life-changing adventure of future planning. Here's how I went about doing it:

1. Based on the information received, I established clear, quantifiable, and doable **goals** for the upcoming holiday season. These objectives acted as a guide for the whole year.

2. Using data on top-performing products, I meticulously vetted my holiday choice of products and made sure I had enough of the most sought-after things in stock.

3. I improved my marketing plan by using the lessons I learnt from consumer feedback to address the worries and preferences of my target audience.

4. I optimized staffing and fulfillment procedures to increase productivity and improve customer service.

5. Continuous Learning: I made a commitment to continued data collection and analysis all year long, not just during the holiday season, after realizing the significance of data and insights. I made sure I never stopped leaning how to continually improve.

Post-Holiday Analysis's Influence

One cannot overestimate the importance of post-holiday review and future planning. It changed my company from being one that merely followed current market conditions to one that actively shaped its future. By utilizing the data and knowledge gained from prior experiences, I was able to position my company for success throughout the year as well as boost performance during the holiday season.

Through this approach, I discovered an essential truth: the past can serve as an effective road map for the future. Post-holiday analysis serves as a platform for strategic development and advancement rather than just a reflection on what has previously happened. It's an approach that has grown to be an essential component of my company and has given me the tools I need to overcome obstacles, make wise decisions, and welcome the limitless possibilities the future brings.

1. I was better able to determine which products had outperformed expectations throughout the holidays and which had fallen short using data analysis. With the use of this knowledge, I was able to choose the right products and manage my inventory for the future year using data.

2. I also combed through customer reviews and feedback, learning important details about their preferences, wants, and trouble issues. This gave me the opportunity to customize my services and raise client satisfaction.

3. The investigation identified several areas that need operational upgrades, from streamlining fulfillment procedures to improving marketing initiatives.

YOUR REALISTIC TO-DO LIST

Post-Holiday Analysis

> ➢ Compile Customers sales data from the most recent holiday season.
> ➢ Examine the gathered data to spot trends, the best-selling items, consumer preferences, and potential areas for development.
> ➢ Review client evaluations and comments in-depth to learn about the experiences and expectations of your customers.

Making Future Plans

> ➢ Based on the knowledge you have been able to gather from the analysis, establish clear, quantifiable goals for the forthcoming Christmas season.
> ➢ Choose your Christmas merchandise carefully, and make sure you have

plenty of the best-selling things on hand and fill in any product gaps.

➤ Adjust your marketing plan to reflect the preferences and problems of your target audience that were discovered through investigation.

➤ Implement operational adjustments to boost effectiveness and customer service, while streamlining staffing and fulfillment procedures.

➤ To stay informed and proactive throughout the year, commit to continual data collecting and analysis rather than simply during the holiday season.

Endeavour to complete the tasks on this list, you'll be well-equipped to perform a post-holiday review and use the knowledge gathered to plan for a successful future. This will guarantee that your company is flexible and sensitive to changing customer demands and market trends.

HOLIDAY HUSTLE

Chapter 8

20 Lucrative Business Start-Up Choices

When the Holiday season comes around, immediately after you receive your monthly wage, does your income stop? Why not think about pursuing a side hustle, which can provide you with additional sources of cash and make your holiday season more enjoyable? Do you want to start the New Year with a smile and enough money to last you for the upcoming months, or do you want to avoid being one of the three-quarters of individuals who find themselves financially pressured once the holiday season ends? These side businesses may be the extra income you've been looking for, whether you're a student, a nursing mother, a father, a businessperson, or an entrepreneur?

The side business you've been looking for could be one of the opportunities listed below. It might not be enough to rely entirely on your salary, pocket money, or maintenance, so check over the supplied business ideas and choose the ones that catch your attention. There are numerous income streams ready to be investigated, and I'm now providing them to you, so don't wait. Consider all the options!

Here are **20** lucrative businesses that you can set up with a minimum amount of money and earn during festive or holiday seasons:

1. Packaging gifts service: During the holiday season, provide specialized gift wrapping services to both individuals and businesses. You may turn a nice profit with inventive packaging and a modest outlay for wrapping supplies.

2. Holiday Decoration Sales: During the festive seasons, locate and sell holiday accents like ornaments, lights, and wreaths online or through pop-up shops.

3. Holiday catering or baking: If you have a knack for cooking, consider opening a business doing either. For gatherings and parties, include seasonal delights like cookies, cakes, and special holiday meals.

4. Arranging an event: Become an event planner who specializes in holiday parties and gatherings by using your organizational skills. Plan the client's décor, catering, and entertainment.

5. Sales of Christmas trees during the holidays, set up a temporary Christmas tree lot. Trees can be purchased from nearby vendors and sold directly to clients.

6. Holiday photography: If you're a talented photographer, consider providing Christmas-themed portrait sessions for individuals, couples, and families searching for treasured holiday pictures.

7. Holiday housekeeping services: For the holidays, a lot of individuals want their homes to be in perfect condition. Start a holiday cleaning business to assist people in getting ready for festive events.

8. Personal Shopping and presents wrapping: Provide clients who are busy with holiday shopping with a personal shopping service where you buy and wrap gifts on their behalf.

9. Creation of Handcrafted items and holiday gifts: Create and market handcrafted holiday-themed crafts online or at regional craft fairs, such as ornaments, candles, and decorations.

10. Services for pet care: During the holidays, a lot of pet owners travel and need trustworthy dog walkers or pet sitters to take care of their four-legged family members.

11. Holiday present shopping support: Provide a service that helps busy people choose and buy the ideal presents for their loved ones. Fees or a portion of the overall gift budget may be requested.

12. Holiday light installation: Assist property owners and businesses with the holiday lighting and ornamentation of their buildings. During the holiday season, you can gain the fundamentals of installation and market your services.

13. Singing or Caroling Telegrams: Offer customized singing telegrams or caroling for holiday events, parties, or special occasions if you have a good singing voice or other musical abilities.

14. Offer snow shoveling services to residents and businesses in locations with snowy winters to keep driveways and pathways clear over the holiday season.

15. Holiday Modification Service: For consumers searching for personalized gifts, personalize holiday accessories like stockings, ornaments, or greeting cards with names, sentiments, or artwork.

16. Start a local gift delivery service: Where you pick up and deliver special deliveries, flowers, and holiday gifts for people or businesses.

17. Christmas light tours: Create and lead guided Christmas light tours in your neighborhood to provide groups and families with a joyous experience.

18. Holiday technical support: If you're tech adept, consider providing on-call technical support to assist individuals in configuring and troubleshooting their brand-new technological gifts.

19. Rent out a variety of "ugly" sweaters with Christmas themes for events or gatherings where visitors are encouraged to wear festive attire.

20. Holiday Plant Maintenance: Provide a plant-sitting service for people who have potted poinsettias or other festive plants. Throughout the season, make sure the plants are well-cared-for, well-watered, and looking their best.

These business concepts can be easily understood and only demand a small initial investment. They give you the chance to increase your income over the holiday season while bringing cheer and holiday cheer to your clients.

"Be prepared to suffer if you don't have anything to offer."

93

You can use the little things you do and the services you provide for others at home to earn money outdoors. Give it to people who feel too lazy to do it as a service. Maximize your skills rather than wasting them. Explore yourself because you contain a gold mine.

Conclusion

Making a Plan for Eternal Success

As we come to an end here in the pages of "Holiday Side Hustle: The Q4 Sales Success Manual for Small Business Owner," I want to leave you with a deep fact that has served as the compass for my entrepreneurial journey: success is not a destination; it is a continual journey.

The numerous ideas, tactics, and lessons that can equip small company owners to prosper during the holiday season and beyond have been covered in the book's chapters. These insights lay the groundwork for your route to success, from analyzing the competitive environment to streamlining product selection, recruiting for optimal performance, and producing amazing client experiences.

But it's important to keep in mind that the trip doesn't finish here. In actuality, it's just the start. The tactics described in these pages can be used year after year; they are timeless practices and ideas that are not specific to a particular holiday season. You may create a route to unending success by consistently committing to improvement, being flexible in the face of change, and maintaining a laser-like focus on your consumers.

Consider going over the insightful information you learned from post-holiday analysis and future planning as you look back on your business journey. Accept the power of customer-centricity, data-driven decision-making, and ongoing learning. Focus on surviving in the opportunities that lie ahead of the future rather than just surviving the obstacles of the present.

Keep in mind that success isn't just determined by revenue or market share; it's also determined by the legacy you leave behind, the long-lasting effect you have, and the relationships you cultivate. Your small business has the capacity to not just endure, but to thrive and make a lasting impression on your sector of the economy and the lives of your clients.

I'll end by urging you to set out on this path with tenacity and unflinching faith in your vision. The busy Christmas season is your opportunity to forge enduring relationships and joyful memories. And when you put the teachings from these pages into practice, you'll discover that success isn't only about getting where you want to go; it's also about appreciating the beauty of the journey.

I wish you a great holiday season, continued success in your business, and limitless chances for the future. Have fun working hard, and may you always have a strong sense of entrepreneurship.

HOLIDAY HUSTLE

9 798862 280241